BJ Ruddy

Pond

BJ Ruddy

Middlebury House Publishing

Pond

To Jean, Connor, and Will
thanks

ISBN # 978-0-9792067-9-5

Middlebury House Publishing
Charleston, SC

Copyright © 2009
BJ Ruddy

All rights reserved, no reproduction or digital distribution of any kind without permission from the author and publisher.

Table of Contents

Here and There	6
Untitled (for significant effect)	7
Pond, Early Morning	9
Happiness Just Might Be	10
Sunset at Pond with Frank O'Hara	11
Selfless Selfishness	12
The Great American Travel Poem	13
Sunbeam	16
Imagine	17
It's Not about Dreams	19
A Poet's Lie	20
Caffeine Dreams	21
Pond at Dawn	22
Sunset Suburbia	23
The Ready Act	24
Just Like the Ocean	25
Exit Poem	26
Coltrane and Conversation	27
Autumn Poem	28
Still Life with Cat	29
Snow Day	30
An Aging Needle Touches Down	31
The Street Jesus	32
Three Generations	33
Zen at the Beach	34
Appearance Reality	35
Interpersonal Relationships	36
An Existential Moment	37
Crackers	38
Boy to Girl	39
In Love in Language	40
Academics	41
Enlightenment at the Y	42
You Me	43

The Morning Sun	44
The Creation Devils	45
Ah, April…	46
And We All Shine On	47
Backyard Blues #3	48
Backyard Blues #4	49
Not So Much Regret	50
Camp Night	52
Considering Road Songs	53
Ghosts	55
The Way	57
The Day after Love	58
The Important Question	59
Sick Day	60
Lunar Cycles	61
Meditation on Music and Sweat	62
At the Movies	64
Movie Preview	65
Love Poem While Cooking	71
Pond	72
Goodbye from Old Southern Church	73
Hello, Master Tiger!	75
Resurrection	77
An Old Set List	78
The Mount Raised Eyes	79
Springtime	80
Jersey Plates	81
We Wandered to the Mountains	82
Haiku for Vermont Brewery	83
Nice	84
Breakfast Contemplation	85
And	86
What Time?	87
Over Somewhere Else's Cup of Coffee	89
Pond Reflection	90
Poem I Wrote in My Head, Was Wonderful, and Was Lost	91

BJ Ruddy

Cutting Back	92
Wisdom	95
Radio	96
Letter to My Friend's Father	98
When I Met the President	99
Tragedy at the Garbage Dump	100
Emily Dickenson's Cell Phone Rings	102
Cigarettes	104
The Corner of King and Calhoun	106
Construction Site	110
The Old Mercedes	111
C	113

"An old pond;
A frog jumps in--
The sound of water."

Matsuo Basho

Here and There

A bald guy walks into a bar
ber shop
says
"I've lost my way"

The barber,
healthy mid-sixties Italian man,
looks over the bald stranger
his younger, thin arms
his trendier, post-college casual
jeans and t-shirt

"Well then, why are you here?"

The silence of snow
hangs and the bald man
leaves so the barber
returns
(as he had no customers)
to his novel

But he only puts it down
after a few unregistered sentences
to wonder what it was
that got him here

Untitled (for significant effect)

What does the morning tell you, poet?

Will there be black crows on fences
badly wintered, in need of paint,
rising from brown grass, unkempt,
and rabbit droppings?
Rusty gate hinges, as foreboding as the crows
staring like the old cranks in the balcony,
cynic puppets mocking Muppets,
are a dare to walk forth without failing –
the assumption that it's just inevitable
is there, too

Or, the light flight of stick cranes
thin and soft in January, still
Buddha amongst the reeds
the gray moody overcast only
highlights their white graze
their easy peace is not noticing you

So what, poet?
Imagine this day real

Will quick crimson-breasted cardinals
ignite in us passionate reasons to breathe
hot Miami nights into freezing Boston lungs?

Or Blue Jays, jamming slow pain,
knowing they'll bite you just as soon
as sing to you
because we're all so cloaked in difference
but blue is the color of blood

Pond

So what will morning bring, poet?

Or, is this winter pond
just brown Ruddy ducks flown south
and bad symbolism?

Pond, Early Morning

Misty steam over the pond
this early morning
geese look like revelers
in a hot tub

Sunrise lights browned reeds
bare trees look brittle
in the still degrees
of January

There's a question of contrasts, too
as I sit, goopy-eyed
with wine-stained lips
soft flannels and sweatshirt
watching from behind glass
attempting identification
with reveling geese or brittle trees

Because maybe I had it
all wrong
and maybe the misty steam
that started all this
is really only lingering remains
of the ghosts of night,
ancestral connections
to the gods, to identity

Ghosts I ignore
thinking too much about geese
who clearly know how to live
amongst such brittle trees

Happiness Just Might Be…

Happiness just might be
the view of a beautiful woman
naked
stealing from bed
and looking back with a sly smile
glowing in the high
that follows early morning love making

It could then be said
that extreme happiness
would be that same woman
returning to bed
nuzzling in winter fox embrace
with gentle touches
leading to one more round

I've always assumed
extremes to be dangerous
but this one
is really tough to argue

Sunset at Pond with Frank O'Hara

I watch the spring orange roll
to clearer blues of eastern night
chilly yet in the low country
still water with some gnats

and so Frank starts rambling
about beautiful subway girls
talk of bars and fat sexy cows
"Buddy," he'd say, "More like
Still Life with Volvo"
and this would hit home

"Ah, come on" I might respond
with faux inflated surprise hurt eyes
but he'd be jittering off
waving cigarettes, accidentally painting
the coming night with beauty
writing of oranges while I
listen to baseball with the pond

Selfless Selfishness

to call these acts selfless
would be the most selfish thing
because it is within my self-interest
to see you smile

and it's true
even Ayn Rand was in love
and love, they say
is blindness
therefore quite subjective
which renders altruism
(let alone objectivism)
complex

and me, alone
angry and pouting

because I can't make you smile

The Great American Travel Poem

What is it to work
and who is to measure accomplishment
when all I can imagine
is going to Peru
with Ginsberg's ghost

I've never been to Peru
but the Lima dive bar
where Allen and I would be
is so vivid
in jungle humidity
down to the sticky counter
stained with local brews
and cigarette burns

There are, of course,
open windows
and the atmospheric earthy wet
green, green, green
outside
while inside
just tilted paintings
of ill-uniformed gorilla generals
and Spanish words

The too-young waitress
eyes whimsical big dreams
at this American poet and me
while broken English from her dark lips
acknowledges our order
of two whiskey sours
and in curt Spanish
she's off, shaking hips like
no American woman ever could

Pond

Rocking back in a paint-chipped stool
ancient turquoise on sturdy wood
I notice American jazz on speakers
with the sound quality
of a late fifties Buick
trumpet lead, some guitar,
and a wild, fluid drummer
riding his snare
like an old long-boarder
rides low, windless waves
that never seem to break

And just like that
Allen and I are on a beach
it's daylight and we're high
(must be ether)
and heading towards this little shed
green wood, Christmas-light sign
we're heading for drinks
but I'm drinking alone
among some sweaty South American laborers
smoking slowly and en masse

The sun is a magnet
that keeps girls in light dresses
at bay
until the moon
comes to reverse the pull
and I'll dance
while Allen
chats up the bus boy
and disappears

Waking up
in some strange back room
to Robitussin and black coffee

BJ Ruddy

Allen nowhere to be seen
I write poems through noon
only to begin again

But really
I'd just miss you
where un-bored nights are peace
a novel to nod off to
while the TV drones low jazz or baseball
the half-full wine glass
never emptied

Sunbeam

I don't know where babies come from
though I suppose I could shed some light,
that first sunbeam that breaks a summer storm,
on how they're made

Because there is no moment
that can't be called the child
of the moment
when she first walked through
green coffee shop doors
on her lunch break
August bright, holding back
its weight

After that –
chain reactions, cells dancing
teenage concert hysteria
all those smiles
all that power
all sparked by a girl
who walked through a door
while I was working

So, I only know babies are natural
and nature
we call "mother"

Imagine

Drifting lazy Sunday couches
something about Saturn's rings
in their gaseous light brilliance
turns the gears of body industry
and somehow the Northern Lights
in crisp, cold, and pure Alaska
are now my ancestral spirits...

To imagine this
is fine
it's dismissible
to believe
sure, why not
(to each his own)

To know this
(though, you know,
people will talk)
is to know ocean
as mother
winter
as old man
time not as father
but patriarch
and matriarch
and the obvious progeny
beauty

But why couldn't we be wrong
and give "Imagine" a spin
so that the day to day keeps going
through cosmic starry nights
which is to say, really, a return
to ancient earth knowing ancestors

Pond

in the Northern Lights
or among the rings of Saturn

Now dazed out of my sleepy couch daze
it's time to see science
in all its intellectual, documented brilliance
as what let me know Saturn
even existed

If there's a return to be had
it's really only to see
that poet and scientist
are not that far removed

BJ Ruddy

It's Not about Dreams

It's not about dreams
you know, but it is
sandwiches in the sand
put into smiles, as if
love was nutrition

And my worth, a click –
no longer "on the books" –
but numbers for my hours
are there with groceries
and cable costs

Which is a breath out
into salt air with soft
voices singing away sirens,
lulling Poseidon, staying
vengeance till tomorrow

Dreams are not what matter
nor do "dream jobs"
but the thinking of poems
little boys and a pretty girl
bring me to dream up

A Poet's Lie

They say poets lie
so Saturday afternoon
drifts into evening
under overcast January
while the book I was reading
slips across my chest
the plot now the stuff
of dreams

To lie down, they're right –
to avoid truth is as impossible
as to claim to know it

For instance,
the twenty-eight year-old girl
who is mother and wife
but girl, here,
extends pianist fingers
jazz Christmas slow
across porcelain villages
New England atop bookshelves
her curves a contrast
to carpentry's angles
letting me, watching,
know her humanity

So truth and imagination
are the view from my bed
looking at a porch,
two empty chairs,
overlooking a windless pond

Oh, the colors?
The colors are up to you

BJ Ruddy

Caffeine Dreams

the stilted in and out anxiety
sort of facing a naked crowd
no fever hallucinations,
beautiful, sweaty, terrifying,
to whirl the wakeful minute hours
into passed time

no, just street swag paranoia
a drizzle without the music-box twinkle
of rain

ten years ago, there was that
humiliating scene at Brian's party
exposed and stared at
the memory vanished somewhere
in the cleanup of Hiroshima
tonight, though, it is back
in emotional landfalls
that, in their winds,
spin beautiful still-life's
and photographs of still, autumn ponds

if time, as various philosophers have considered,
does not exist (in the linear sense)
then what can bring peace, tonight,
but the knowledge that tomorrow's exhaustion
will bring a heavy head down on the couch
by the third inning?

though, it must here be considered,
as many have said
tomorrow never comes

Pond at Dawn

Pond at dawn
cold gator bites
the day before February

These papers
will earn letters
later

The inclination
is to daydream
as coffee is sun
through a big fog
which bites like the cold
of a pond at dawn
the day before February

Lazily observing
the curse of an autumn birth
it's the evergreens I admire

Sunset Suburbia

Lay down, suburbia,
for the watercolors up over our roofs
are tinted sky blue
where electricity is cloud condensed
and the picture's clarity
is enough to bring thoughts…

This pond to my right
knows about natural decoration
the importance of function and place
and like me
only lies still in reflection
mirroring the view
to you…

And what is it, now,
that brings us together
in contemplation of nature
unearthing wisdom of self
for a gentle exhale
of what can only be deemed
the troubles of the day?

Whatever that is
I can only hope,
looking up as the orange fades
more purple by the minute,
it is not Caesar ladder climbing
just to celebrate our elite height
and only the actualizing
of a tree-fort's potential

The Ready Act

I'm not ready
to free myself
from needs and wants

But the child in line
is never ready
for his first roller coaster

The young soldier
high above his destination
is not ready to jump

Nor are two lovers,
awed by a nursing babe,
ready for the first fever

Everyday,
people act –
here I am among you

BJ Ruddy

Just Like the Ocean

wet morning boardwalk
low tide humid stillness
brings memories
of all those hung-over adolescences

the day went on
through Magic Kingdom fairy tales
and everybody smiled
just because
we could

it's not lonely
it's terribly lonely

but what's funny is the feeling
so similar
I just don't have to puke
and the boys
sleeping out the exhausted lunacies
of adult potential

"what's going on?" asked the boy to the ocean
"ha, ha, ha!" the ocean laughed back

the light waves washed
and Om was clear enough
to me

Exit Poem

It's not so easy
to refuse you
so no becomes my word
for others

and I become that person
reliably refusing
while to you
it's surrender

this is the work of Sartre
in daily coffee
I'm just not sure
I care

BJ Ruddy

Coltrane and Conversation

Funny how the stumbling
        tumbles
into turbulence……is there any
home bass still beat
rhythm, is there rhythm?

These conversations hold slow
breaths where I can
see your lipstick every eye line
every tongue turned
into words that build
weaving and weaving
to what   to where
and here we talk under all this moving
louder   faster   harder

And the whole thing comes to pass
breath catch…..is there a snare still tapping
bass….anything at all?

Autumn Poem

Sometimes
ancient poets from far away lands
are closest to my thoughts…
and in a déjà vu of sorts
I unfold my eyelids
to view autumn   happening

In the breathless still
of one orange maple leaf
floating down – a death dance –
from somewhere higher…
my past is clean
I can see

But, I know, these moments
of brilliance
are just that –
and this is, after all, sometimes

And me
I'm fortunate

Still Life with Cat

Darkness is not boring
But what could be less interesting
than heat
Drenched in humidity
Spun through a fan
Almost as thick as mist
Life-like in the moonlight
While the cat stays so still

Snow Day

T.V. scenes passing
eyes fading
sleep to dream? oh, you
next to close by speaking
what snowy day peace
let me sleep here with you your voice
sounding in and out
as the world
shuts
down

sleep

An Aging Needle Touches Down

An aging needle touches down
deep in the night
on soft, worn grooves
a warm, fuzzy hiss illuminates the silence
white noise, drowning out the world
or music
the occasional crackle, and then
those low tone, easy bass beats
a rolling wisp to snare, the stage set
a horn to blow…

In another corner, a face, speakers
and with windows all around
the isolation of the world
is a closed book on my knee
and sleep is broken glass

The Street Jesus
For MM

I saw a collage

graphic design skills
were obvious

faces, faces, faces
Ha! All one face!
smile, howl, awe

even cool

red brown shading effects
one hip seventies-style
yellow-brown shirt

The Street Jesus
is his nickname
I used to know him
as Matt

It's good to see
the brightness
of his smile

as it reminds me
of the way
he kept rhythm

Three Generations

Circles shape memories
but compacts break
just as easily
when dropped
and intentions
carry circles of their own

The grandson on your porch
confessions were easy
in Jersey shore summer
but the adolescent wish
to know her as you did –
another kind of compact –
has only just occurred to me

Zen at the Beach

now a month or so
that ice cream truck music boxes
crank circus themes for our evening ears

and with half a wave
to some girls I've taught
I lost my glasses to the ocean
and worried, under an indifferent sun
in unknowing humidity
while the constantly moving ocean
washed me,
about cost

this could, I suppose, have
something to do with perspective
the ocean washing away
what I use to see clearly
only to give me the blindness
to see clearly

is life so like poems
or some faux-Eastern philosophy?

regardless, with a thought to Amy Tan
I considered my own *nengkan*
and with Zen smiles
continued to body surf with my son

the waves, that day, were great!

Appearance Reality

in humid sunrise
the order of a freshly cut lawn,
edging, trimmed flowers, and cedar mulch
is misleading

because inside
the carpet is stained
clothes are strewn about
and the bathroom sink
is inaccessible

signs are popping up outside, though –
between sidewalk cracks
rogue grass is attempting hegemony
and summer has done its share
to the white wooden fence

plus, opening the garage
is risking exposure
like the high mileage
on the car

today, I watch the pond take light
while fog hangs as spirits
her body cremated, I can't put a place
on my grandmother
so she's everywhere
and isn't fooled by the lawn

Interpersonal Relationships

It wasn't so nice
to tell Tommy
he wasn't the sharpest tool in the shed
he knew that meant stupid
which translated to
he couldn't play standard
academic games
as well as others
which insinuates there are other intelligences
like Mr. Gardner's been praised
for discovering while –
it's important to note –
at Harvard

Then again
it wasn't so nice
of Tommy
to call Jenny a nerd
she knew that meant goody-goody
which translated to
she didn't buy into
social norms of collective mediocrity
insinuating she was a master
of real individuality and self-interest
like she thought
when she wasn't so nice
to Tommy

BJ Ruddy

An Existential Moment

"One always dies too soon - or too late. And yet one's whole life is complete at that moment, with a line drawn neatly under it, ready for the summing up. You are - your life, and nothing else."
- *Inez, from Jean Paul Sartre's* No Exit

The little boy
with the tennis racket
swings a wild smile
by a path
by a pond

The driver of the
Chevy pickup
smiles almost home thoughts
wife with child
rounds a curve

At the moment
of impact, smiles
crossed two faces
only too
soon to fade

Crackers

crackers with habanera pepper cheese
pepperoni and water
at 4:30 in the afternoon
are different than the usual
late night snacking with beer

but they're good this way

left field thunderstorms
delay games
but the reflected sunset's orange
makes waiting beautiful
even if the Yankees end up losing

morning exercise routines
are meditations
a perfect combination
between the task at hand
and yesterday's reflection
hand-walking the toddler
that is today's anticipation

a couple of weeks left
of summer vacation
boys read, draw, sing
and snack with me

to be angry might be crazy
but we're smile junkies
who lack sufficient funds
and I have the nerve
to write poems

BJ Ruddy

Boy to Girl

If I'm not there
to let the water through
(light sand through a sieve)
attempting to hold it all back
you'll drown faster
anyway
maybe the force alone
will knock you out
and suffering will be minimal
but I guess that's not really
getting what we deserve

In Love in Language

your heart drops
from wise cherry trees

waiting mouths
are young lovers below

and the wind
Kurt Cobain's guitar

makes language
so insignificant

Academics

You're not obliged
to read all
of these books

You cup!
There are many
liquids available

and walks by houses…
what's the health
you are seeking?

Memories are books
and the symbolism
of an old photograph

There are paths and water
Best to know
your footing

Enlightenment at the Y

There has always been a certain Zen
in morning exercise
whether it be the pretty seventy degree
spring or cooling autumn morning run
or just time at the local YMCA
there's a waking in the accomplishment
of ritual
and it's why I leave the iPod home

Prayer had left my life
I have reasons and excuses
depending on which mirror
I'm in front of
the typical Catholic corruption
all the way to the opiate of the masses
sort of stuff

But this morning
there was this man
in between reps
on the press machine
arms folded, head bowed
there was no condescension
no opiate, no new addiction
just Buddha solemnity

I knew why I once prayed
and why I'll have to find
my own way back

You Me

you're somewhere out there
among the robots and atomic gardening
but I know you want
to be outside, out back
under a cool night's song
a dark and stormy head
falling for timeless rivers
with me

The Morning Sun

The morning sun
Is a hazy science fiction beacon
Rising consistent and slow
Over developments – or destructions –
The eyes of adolescent hallucinogenic drugs
Watch in awe
The eyes of the American attempting Buddha
Watch in awe
As a plane flies across this vision
Of the morning sun

The Creation Devils

framing the madness…yes, pin the murder –
fight another day so it can be
cooped up in bedrooms, the child is
protected we say, so it can be
the fault of society, of government, of parents
those creation devils, sirens of carnal earth
so it can be that
things fall apart from the inside, too

"they've made it easy to make these choices"
the man in tie, the woman in pencil skirt
without breakfast or affection, affectation
wanders out the door, to car, to noise
these are bullets, heavy lead,
melted down by thousand degree psychology
poured to form, easy choices

to pick up the pieces, as some say,
is regeneration, an organic option,
the only thing to do…tomorrow

one walk, father, mother, children –
one sun, one moon, light provided
dim universe beating, exploding,
regenerating – perceptions of the creation devils
things fall apart and life goes on

there's a CD in my collection
entitled *Demolition as an Art*
and this applies
because action hasn't been mentioned
much at all

Ah, April…

in the warm morning mist, spring
a French-kiss for existence and
as all kisses flush forward
every day returns

this is spring and you are naked
ready to be kissed with sun
and thunderstorms by open windows
fingers graze as lightly
as the white sheets that drape
sun-burnt legs

lawn care is muddy foreplay
dually grasping the familial whole
as the boys can hear the wind
humid air urges us
in the ways of breathing

I believe in new beginnings
amidst too many raven reminders
of self-indulgent winter haunts
for now, to child dandelion sniff
window breezes above you
shower fresh and always young
I can finally exhale November
and in warm morning moist spring
French-kiss existence
on your lips

BJ Ruddy

And We All Shine On…

The basket weaver
hunches low under an old oak
and the southern moss
must drape like palms to the basket
like her eyes that I can't see
The side of Route 17
is loud with exhaust and humidity
but there are other weavers
along this road
from Charleston through Mount Pleasant
and there must be enough customers
so she weaves on

A twenty-eight year old blond girl
crosses long, tan legs
at a picnic table under an old pine
delicate in sips from a bottle
eyes taking in little boys
at play
She does consider
what could have been
had she not taken each road
to this picnic table
but considerations won't affect happiness
so she smiles on

Backyard Blues #3

We were out back
till at least two
pretzels and guitars
Kate went down around eleven
Jay disappeared around one
but we couldn't stop laughing
and so we stumbled inside
from a mild August night
for nachos
my late night forte
cheese glopped on beans and veggies
crunchy chips fill warm, drunken bellies
steadying the head
for what reality may come
when woken hours later
to greet another day
a tired, happy haze
and vague recollections
piece together the puzzle
all we ever need
to get to the beach
and let the rolling waves
rock us till Sunday sleep

BJ Ruddy

Backyard Blues #4

watching the moon
arc across the night

time passes without
thinking of clocks

hearty laughs, swigs,
voices with guitars

it's almost time
to wake up

hungry bellies
want donuts, dad

Not So Much Regret, But...
for WL

we had wanted to fly
over summer

(without ever formulating
the thought)

suspended in
mirages

that sat well
with us

sitting in lawn chairs
at sunrise

when they broke up
youth ended

and like youth
they tried again

but we all knew
it wasn't the same

the mirages wore off
dry reality

was time to cut ties
like boys' long hair

BJ Ruddy

we still want to fly
over summer

now we just accept
the fall

Camp Night

Around the campfire
midnight passes and I still hear
the pretty girl's Joplin sad voice
(but now, no more guitars,
no other voices)
walking her to a moonlit bathroom
stumbling in drunken freedom
from a morning alarm

Marinated in bug spray
sleepy children fight nodding off
to sing along and burn
marshmallows
knowing somehow these adults
feel this ritual important
discipline hasn't been necessary
since before dinner

BJ Ruddy

Considering Road Songs

If these thoughts are a truant's
then let me get coincidence and apologies
out of the way
while I persist without consciousness
of conscientiousness
in this walk through our home

You'll understand there are miles here
many road songs of exhaustion and persistence
and from "Moonlight Mile" to "Melissa"
we still like "Thunder Road"
each stain on rugs that wear as tired tires
is the routine of morning coffee
equally overlooked as passing remarks
are clues to our secret lives that
I'm not confident in following

But on goes the walk past windows
where the black cat smiles in out-of-character adoration
while friends giggle stumble out the door
and reckless fantasy plays real enough
for me

Circling fans and dryers hum lullabies
while mother kisses make human
the father god, unconscious of his power,
my breath is choked in laughter
wishing off the duties of the day, knowing
the great truth of finishing this walk
is just another mirror squared off in bathrooms

but back in our bedroom
it's my side without moonlight or the pond
whose parasites and muddy depth

Pond

remind me of my truancy
so I'll open this window to the thunder
and lie down in this white bed naked
next to you, just to see

We weren't built
to wait in baited anticipation
for the spoils of sea merchants
breathing is unconscious
yet it's up to us to take deep breaths
in matters of health

Ghosts

Ghosts in the rearview mirror
and hushed whisper tornadoes
through hollow hallways,
staircase disaster climbs
just hands under the hot water
again a-breathless-gain…

All the shadows of Saturday
spring up in weekday wonder
good intentions good for shaming
while windy beach sandwiches
are signs of age
for late-afternoon love-making
with young eyes
while experience only gazes
in overdriven guitar memories
of cigarettes in the morning
and the enjoyment of loneliness…

Can the stars be blasted like a building
(detonate just to create)
because Scorpio can't sting
and all the drugs don't work
anymore…

There's a young beauty with a vacuum
left to repeat patterns over again
all across already worn rugs
and there's my beautiful grandmother
gripped by a million circus audience eyes
Fenway beams blocking a view of the game…

But young eyes say it's magic
young eyes say it will fly

Pond

and that star-crossed lovers
can love deeply, damning the consequences,
just two kids in August New Jersey
sipping coffee that's a butterfly's flight
to the debt of years…

From mirrors of improbability,
the tired passport stamps journal
wisdom with nearly dry pens
fearing experience was a marathon
because there's not a lot of figuring
left to do, just Over-Soul and a greedy ostrich
with wisdom selling sea songs,
grandmother echoes, we get the point…

Ghosts are jamming signals
but if we keep tweaking the dial,
they'll shut up, no WWII code-breakers
and clearly unsure of pirate radio power,
Excalibur is a strong weapon
if held by the true king,
God and ancestors, the ocean and children,
silenced to the white noise
that young eyes drive on through
tweaking, tweaking, tweaking
until the perfect sound just plays
on and on and on…

And maybe it's the Jersey Shore
and how very far away it seems
when you get too old to cry,
Cobain's pain can't cut it anymore…

The Way

warm winds
rain heavy clouds
over sunrise

the pond,
shadowed, is
blown from all directions

a man running
glides past
a young tree bending

The Day after Love

Still cold
spring turns a phrase
with moisture

(the lover's quarrel
had been winter's
still dry cool)

Helios has a say
but the seasons
don't leave
each other's
side

considering tides
spring is confidence
a balance
of power
after all

BJ Ruddy

The Important Question

Bearing the cross
is, I suppose,
just another choice

To let it lie
somewhere roadside
is a choice

So why embark
on I-95
way up in Houltin, Maine,
heading down
to Miami, Florida,
picking up crosses
when the extra weight
just slows the journey
…and with gas so costly?

Well, slow and steady
and all that
could be considered
but, really,
how much freedom
do we want?

Sick Day

left work today
after only an hour
Will, who's four, felt sick

I left assignments
and took papers
there are movies for Will

blankets for both
a sleepy winter sun
warming our little world

I don't know
if Will is sick or smart
and I don't really care

Lunar Cycles

Fading moons
they only seem
to disappear
crescent, half,
harvest orange
they will
again
fill the sky

A child's eyes
only seem to disappear
watching others
until staring
into other eyes
making a child

Which makes one think of innocence
because the moon is just an illusion
always, really, being full
of itself

Meditation on Music and Sweat
because Nick was worried about losing a finger

To listen to live music
in old theaters off Broadway
when our sweat smelled different
and our feet tapped not to the beats
of subways underneath, but to hearts
in the monitors singing
into ticket-stub smiles,
later to be stuck in mirrors
and albums, drawers, and notebooks
but first warm and wet
in perfect jeans, where the feeling
never fades away

Once upon a howl
beat poets hung smoky thoughts
over wordless improvisations
while sugar packets
in black plastic holders
dripped with spilled milk

And were we so different
at two a.m. coffee house diners
with stained teeth and hormones
dodging winter with speedy sweat
Jane's Addiction trance rhythms
lulling speech down mountains
into sunrise staggers home

Sweat
night movies and too much coffee
nothing to dull the edge
when punk rock lacks the sense
and odd time indie-rock

is the only sound worth breathing
its cynicism genuine to time
and the abstractions of reality

Sigh…
sweat against a July guitar
low-toned, its forest green finish
holds the moon like a young girl's
harvest eyes, looking to her kiss,
moments away from someone's dad
and the beautiful awkwardness
of the ride home, where
whatever plays on the radio
is the greatest song of all time
and will forever invoke
the sweat of this moment
the hazy traffic lights and neon businesses,
fast food, banks, and gas stations,
fading behind in a white noise hum
of distortion pretty speakers,
whispering friends and the stoic driver dad

"I'm breathing" she knows
she knows that she's alive

At the Movies

Ah yes, Zen…

At the movies with the kids,
the wise, computer animated ancient turtle
a kung-fu master
said "the present is a gift
that's why it's called 'present'"
then he pulled the "it's my time" line
and we find his great scroll was blank
that there are no answers
but the ones you know from within
or, of course, those you create,
but…

At the movies, this all seems great
as it does in pre-dawn sips of coffee
in the bathroom
or late at night listening to west coast baseball
but in summer traffic
in brotherly battles where the blood of war
is spilled cranberry juice on a new tan carpet
when exam grades are due
and the parent of Satan incarnate
(daddy's little girl)
is questioning the D
I *gave* his princess…

Ah yes, Zen
it's times like these
I think
what a load of crap

BJ Ruddy

Movie Preview
for Jean

You watch movie previews
in soft summer pajamas,
holding the hopes promised
in hooks and lines and scenery –
the happy ending could exist, of course,
so the habit is addictive
and I am helplessly drawn in…

As the lime green screen fills our gray rectangle,
the comfort washes clean sheet warm –
over us –
so that only what's approved of for all audiences
will be shown

It might as well be a View Askew production
(but, really, that's only due to locale
and, probably, Smith's crutch
of a happy ending amidst all
that is emotionally trying)
so the company emblem is the next electric wave
teasing our eyes, always at the ready in anticipation
while some studio chicanery in surround sound
fades to the first scene

The background information always comes first
and as a moderate theme builds
in only strings and woodwinds
there is a young, lost looking male
of some indiscriminate, post-adolescent age
walking a beach
and over the music, an Omniscient narrator with a deep voice
articulates phrases like
        "He was stuck in the lost roles of teenage wastelands

Pond

    that the onset of adulthood had not yet shattered"
That's catchy
and there are more along these lines
like:
    "Escapism and frustration with college
    had beaten down all he once dreamed about"
leading up to the inevitable
    "Until one day…she walked through the door"
The music changes, teasing in up-tempo pep,
leading to the full theme

Quick cut to a glass and green Starbucks,
mini-mall New Jersey suburbia
then a quick moving pan inside
to some indistinct employee's point of view
(which we assume to be that of the young man from the beach)
of a striking young beauty
who, at angles, is centered in refracted sunlight
suggesting to us purity, but one that's weathered experience

As she approaches the counter she is
the focal concentration of faux-amateur camera work
made to appear like this would happen everyday
to any of us watching
the celestial princess promised to all good boys
in Kindergarten fairy-tales

Here, the music stops in a sharp break,
timed perfectly with the camera cut to her
dropping of keys and purse on the counter, lightly,
while her wide-eyed smile and a simple "Hey" –
emphasized greatly in the absence of all sound –
radiate over the rising, now piano-lead theme

That's all we get of their meeting
there is a quick cut to the two characters smiling loudly
with the fresh energy of new life

and while the theme hits a mighty crescendo,
the camera is moving in circles around them
so it appears that we are surrounding
their blooming, powerful, immediate love
while they walk beaches, New York City streets,
and in and out of Jersey shore bars

The narrator is cluing us in:
    "All he'd ever needed was in that coffee shop
    and this customer was going to change his life forever"

We expect the impending cut to silence
but, nonetheless, our hearts still drop
(as they do every time)
as the camera and music –
milliseconds ago dancing in brilliant movement –
screech to a cartoon halt and center on her face
    "I'm pregnant"

The poignant stillness is perfect

A moderate version of the previous theme's intensity
plays over scenes of her growing belly,
doctor's visits and Mexican restaurants,
letting us know that these characters are going to try
and suggesting, clearly, that other
(perhaps more rational, thus boring) people
would not

Interspersed here with a progressive, explanatory narration –
with deep, clearly annunciated phrases like
    "He wanted something to live for
    and now he was going to have just that" –
are great one-liners placed ever-so-perfectly
throughout the sneak-peeks
like her cynical yet oddly tender
    "Hey, you did this to me – deal with it"

Pond

           (while she smiles girlishly in confident surrender)
and carefully laid suggestions that they must work hard
to truly accomplish the task ahead
as when he says
        "I'll have my degree in another year
        so we just have to make it till then"
and we understand these are the words of a young man
who clearly has no idea of what to expect
and applaud the carefully chosen diction

The music deepens (to something near E minor)
only momentarily, we predict, as even though
we haven't been checking watches,
a sense that the preview –
our snippet into the life of these two young lovers
who must overcome a challenging obstacle
and work through the emotions of love
under the duress of growing into adults
perhaps faster than they otherwise would have –
is coming to a close

But first we must see her crying
through an intentionally unsteady lens
while the room is shadowed
to the point where we get only a maroon, brown impression
(contrasting significantly with the previous brightness)

We must also see him slamming a door
and throwing on a baseball cap
(which we assume to be symbolic of fading youth)
while as quick as that motion he's with guys
(his old friends, we know)
considering his options and what it truly means
to give up or to give in
and we're given the smallest of hints to his decision
when he says
        "I love her"

BJ Ruddy

There is one more cut to silence
as his eyes flash open from what must have been midnight sleep
to her voice off screen
> "Um, there's a dead mouse on the floor...
> and I think I'm in labor"

So, of course, this is followed by the rising theme
and the two of them walking side by side
into a thunder-echoing New Jersey hospital
doctors and nurses glaring while she walks strong
(so we know she's the tough cookie of the two)
and he looks ever-so-determined,
trying to play the man he doesn't yet know how to be

The music resolves and she is pushing
with nurses and shadows under florescent lighting
the camera as unsteady as ever
(so we know the bumpy cinematography will be a key element,
potentially symbolic of the couple's bumpy road)
while the narrator speaks of all they'll have to face
of all they'll have to overcome
to realize their ultimate destiny of being together
and raising a child
> "They both knew they needed something
> and it was going to take them both
> to make that something great"

There is a soft fade to the young mother with her baby
both exhausted from the trauma of birth
and the young father staring with a similar exhaustion in his eyes
(though we know it's more of a terrified stupor)

Just before the screen fades to black and the music recedes
the young father, hovering above his new family,
plants a kiss on the young mother's forehead
(both of them eying their resting child)

Pond

and says:
> "We're going to do this,
> no matter how much work it takes,
> I know we'll pull it off"

and we are touched only briefly as,
while the rating and production information appear
over the blackened screen as soft as a low-tide wave,
we hear her final lines of the preview:
> "Will *we*?
> Because it seems like I've been doing all the *work*
> for this kid so far!"

As a less commanding voice informs us that
this film will be in theaters August 18th,
and we sit back, curling into soft-couch comfort
and each other's arms,
we are assured that these two young lovers
will work and love through any struggle
with honest laughter
and the convictions of true devotion
to life for its own sake

We probably won't watch this one,
knowing the story as well as we do.

BJ Ruddy

Love Poem While Cooking

Night's cool breath
        light on my bare feet
        against the warm grill
                that still feels like August

Lost teenage car songs
        rumble low in distant excitement

Calm,
turn the chicken
tend the peppers
hear rolling jazz drums
        build

While the boys drift off to sleep
I await her return

Pond

pond is still
must be no wind

pond is choppy
east wind, some rain

pond drinks rain
becomes full, overflows

pond stares up at sun
eyes reflecting light

BJ Ruddy

Goodbye from Old Southern Church

Holding the white robes back
the alter boy bears the cross,
leading the procession of peers
through the humid white tunnel
of aged plaster,
arching over similar pillars
steeping up from hardwood indifference
to the weight.
Outside unstained windows,
Spanish moss drapes broken brick
footpaths,
dodging graves from the dawn of America
and the wet spring dusk kisses everyone inside
with sweat's glaze,
the incense-strong smell of damp dirt.
Hymns and prayers go through adolescent ears,
some fall off their tongues
with the passion of a reading assignment
first period, Monday morning:
their minds are here, though,
in this church,
mindful as this day
is supposed to be the crossroads
they've waited so long for.
And so it is accepted,
like the hymns and prayers,
but with immediacy so much more appealing
to adolescent America
that the day will be as important
as they've been told.
And in this old southern church,
they'll stir up their memories
and make them so, so special
their education complete, now

Pond

they know the show.
Proceeding out, chatter ensues:
what's going on tonight?
Into the fading light, all the way
through the dawning of the light,
walk now along this feeble path
and realize that what the preacher said
about not wasting life
is good advice,
because all of us do, kids.
All of us do.

BJ Ruddy

Hello, Master Tiger!

loneliness and wistful thoughts
        on karma

squandering days
in traffic jam meditations
the fathoms of cost
bumper dent

nobody sorry in the end
        just begin
hang from cliffs and taste
        the strawberry

beautiful completion

a man walks into a bar
lays down his credit card
        and pays

a man walks into a bar
drinks and smokes and laughs
        and pays

New Jersey stinks in nicotine mothers
wandering thieving midnight
under casino suns
        belly mounds starving
        for emptiness

drugs, sex – "What's your vice, man?"
American dollar dreams

mean, mean, mean
what's it mean

Pond

to be so full
so incomplete?

pregnancy pinching skin
paper bagged weight

EMPTY ME!
EMPTY ME!

Master Tiger
Mr. President
father mother brother neighbor friend lover child teacher student
colleague enemy

I am untying these old shoes
untying in constant expulsion
I am disconnecting

sweet nothingness
sweet completeness

I am letting go
Hello, Master Tiger!

BJ Ruddy

Resurrection

Unspoken conversation dances
candles, breath, wind and God
"between the lines" they say
can the road repair (like always)
in Florida spring, Good Friday,
full moon hangs on Christmas tree sky
over bright mini-mall brilliance
saviors die spent
descendents of hand-washing Pilot

We pass Disney World
for Tampa, spring training,
the rains hang like last night's moon
Poseidon on our hero tails
and all we get are Yankee errors
down six to nothing after one
and after only three the game is called
too much rain, too much rain

We're drenched, we strip on the highway
a nearly naked drive to Jacksonville
passing Disney World again
rebuilding smiles from demolished truths
the boredom of escape
just to taste NYC Italian cooking
red wine and the dry warmth of conversation

Wake to humid Easter Sunday
road repair and missing pieces ignored
rise, savior, rise

An Old Set List
for Brian, Kevin, and Matt

almost time for new beginnings
each day pushing and crossing
one hundred degrees, daredevil
teenagers on bikes across Route 35
for nothing more than gummy bears
and music-shop legends

anxiety is books and planners
on the table highlighted
by windows drenched
in humidity

what impression have I left
letting days roll away
reading or injecting online
morphine in air conditioned rooms

a set list from twelve years ago
Brian remembered most songs
I couldn't hear them all
but I remember getting there
and playing for those dates
never working, never writing,
just playing
under the Shark River inlet moon

good days

good days are different now
though identity is still accidental
heading back to college
heading back to work
here I am

BJ Ruddy

The Mount Raised Eyes

The Mount raised eyes
to subservience and fear
the human born
no Atlantis genius
just cruel parents
watching little eyes
go from scared to cold
to fight disillusioned wars
in the blindness of loneliness
pass the buck
it's what we call holy and
responsibility's absurd, anyway

Springtime

These days, spring rides severe thunderstorm warnings over humid ambiguity – the blankets are off now and we stand before unforgiving crowds in our ugliest underwear...

But it's still spring, the rising phoenix, and we only hope the memories of our burnt winter selves are there to stare back from mirrors, not glanced at, but stared into, so this – this thing, this spring – will be the birth that's gone so long unremembered and clearly unplanned, however oft dreamed of...

Forgotten autumns are the ability of man, now is the energy of youth, the strength of adolescence, the wisdom of the elder and the toddler, the rambling meaning and meaninglessness of an idealistic poet's mouth moving, exhaust breath, internal pistons slowed in the sludge of oil unchanged that is age...

So, spring, again, is alive...

We'll see...

Jersey Plates

Jersey plates
some awful nostalgia

smells of the inlet
July sunsets

these plates of mine
will hang suspended

on low-country walls
to rust in peace

listening to "No Surrender"
or old friends

seeing Jersey plates
is a quick smile

brown roots really do
nourish bright petals

We Wandered to the Mountains

we wandered to the mountains
no brilliance in the wind, no over-soul inspiration
just urine
and man's progress in measuring the body
we took a picture
not of a Vermont valley in late fall
but of our faces
and went to dinner
garlic and conversation
was veiled desperation
as adolescence died

BJ Ruddy

Haiku for Vermont Brewery

Friends, porch, summer night
Cicadas, smiling voices,
Moon's hocus-pocus

Nice

To eat chips and salsa
to drink a few
Mexican beers
to sit with you
under a summer moon
and laugh about
rainy days
would be nice…

BJ Ruddy

Breakfast Contemplation

One cannot help
catching his reflection
in a bowl of instant oatmeal
staring down at
brown mush that
is delicious still

One can only
prepare grinds and water
the night before
just to suppose
coffee five minutes later
is no different

And

Milk & honey, cats & bees
dollars for the girls & boys
sheetrock's got some holes
carpets cover but soak stains
anyway

       "Mister, please, this & that"
       "Of course, but costs…"
       "Drowning cats"
       "Of course, but water ebbs & flows"
       "Mister, years, my record, days"
       "Of course, minutes, reality, the way"

There is no such thing as I (well…)
a country bleeds, ice cream's free
some control of flower growth
some idea of love or God
of present absent father mortgaged children
Marx & Darwin making men
toys for all the smiling youth
comic ballads bending high E tears
FAIL in whose eyes, Baby Blue
EXIST & fall asleep under p.m. pills & pens
no one's there to see you…

BJ Ruddy

What Time?

A friend is disappointed in her friends
except for her husband
who happens to be a great friend
but a bad husband

What has to be done –
dare the earth's ancient findings
sans excavation tools, the treasure's
where the mind body is

A lot of this is bad TV and awkward silence
the bathroom (one light burnt out) mirror
says of course not, these things we know
and we fought with best intentions
kids and kisses and love while it lasted

Seeking to switch roles
my friend looks for herself in others
to be what she hasn't been
with an ostrich's shoulder awareness
of greener pastures and weeds

All the while, minding dreams
whispered voices God, no surprises
sandlot rulebook says just have fun
and indulge the greatest heroes
as everything we need is poison, too

There are other springtime train rides, they say
but the inability to be sure on this matter
makes desperation so naturally plausible

I will fight no more forever, right?
but there was fighting done

Pond

so starting over does not always allow
leaving behind

My friend talks and I watch children swimming
and clocks, pretty girls and youth flexing,
getting more sun burnt by the minute

BJ Ruddy

Over Somewhere Else's Cup of Coffee

Over somewhere else's cup of coffee
stormy winds push through windows
and the muggy still, the sleeping boy
are momentarily riled

I hadn't really been reading
my wife in the store,
I enjoying breezes
in a Sunday doze
that parking lots can offer
under shady trees, spring green

This is the anti-Steinbeck
plastic-pushing middle class America
that I'm resting among
that my son's dreaming in
and dozing only so long
as to consider poems
I'm still young enough to write

Well, I'm still young enough to smile
with arrogant superiority
that is, in my gentle dozing,
completely self-deprecating

and I have learned something

Pond Reflection

The history of the pond
       (I like to think)
is something like the river
of Vasudeva, the ferryman

(I know – or think –
it was really man made
five or so years ago
when they built this development)

But, when you consider fate
this pond was always
meant to be
here

And so I look at it
(there's a slight breeze today)
and know
I, too
am here

Poem I Wrote in My Head, Was Wonderful, and Was Lost

There were lines like

> *She was the lost lady of Loch Ness*
> *Whose fragility was the morning fog*
> *Exploring still water's glass*
> *Disturbing the universe with a finger's gentile prod*

There were more along those…lines
But they're gone

The moment was nice, too
It was almost midnight
And following the bliss of sex
And a slight wine buzz
Lying down and staring up at the ceiling fan
Noticing dust buildup, pondering what *perpetual* might be
There was the still air-conditioned cool
And I thought of the muggy crickets and the sound
I couldn't hear as they shouted with frogs
Nocturnal fowl joining in at random
And I knew I was missing the party of the week
Because I'd shut my own windows
To the life that chose to be alive around me
Smiling with a cynical look to an imaginary mirror
I considered the symbolism therein
And knew its truth

It was a pretty good poem,
But writing it without a computer
Without a notepad
In bed next to a beautiful, however much asleep, woman
That was true
Because it really is about the journey…

Cutting Back

On the morning of the third day
half a summer past
the idea of immeasurable
comes to me and stabs
as a secret sin

For the man who knows indulgences
regret is never enough

But the last two days
will stick
like cigarette smoke in humid rain
and how that smell always brings
seventeen
I will dig these days up

I was weeding
fingernails brown red clay soil stained
the grooves of the shovel
worked wood
knowledgeable to callused palms
poles away from the underground
of all night raves
or good punk rock

A thunderstorm was approaching
the boys went in for a snack
but I kept chopping roots
the organic wet smell an aphrodisiac
I was not the modern American
I was the uncivilized man
who knew what his hands could do
trimming, cutting back
so fresh growth might have a chance

BJ Ruddy

in this Gettysburg of flower beds
digging deep ravines
God, the obsessively particular artist
churning soil, raking wet muck
and moist green stems, leaves
bleeding an orgasm of water
masochistic plant life
sadistic god-man me
organizing man's view of perfection
out of natural chaos
so that invading grass might know its place

All the while, rain began to fall
on my dirt-speckled and sweaty back
and thunder rumbled closer
cracking louder and louder
as my hand-shovel broke back
more branches, unearthed
more roots, and drew
more lines

I was beginning to understand symmetry
when lightening said take a break
and rain poured down
I couldn't tell if this was the sky's release
after watching the erotica of my gardening
or God offering redemption
to me
like I was some lost character
in an OK film

When the rain let up
I finished my job in the July drizzle
Whitman proud of my work
and no longer asking questions
as admiration of my dirty body
muscles more visible than ever before

Pond

needs no philosophy or aesthetic standards

That afternoon
I understood breath and beauty

You were getting your hair cut
while I worked the flower bed
that surrounds the perimeter of our house
and we later spoke of our own potential
while making love

The next day I mowed the lawn
an instant addict
and again observed the strength
of my body
and the power of growth
in cutting

Wisdom

Amidst plans for the beach
looming thunderstorms on computer
and TV blue tint predictions
blue sky actually blaring outside
Will asks what I'm doing
to which I reply
"Writing a poem"

"Oh," he says, as this is
a perfectly acceptable answer
"Well, what are we doing today?"

"I'm not sure," I say,
"The beach might be out
because they say it might rain"

"Oh, well, then we
don't have to go to the beach"

And off he goes
reporting the news to Connor
fine with whatever the natural world
has to offer his four year old self

He knows Zen
without the hindrance
of knowing the word for it

Radio
Remembering WHTG 106.3, Eatontown, NJ

we used to listen to the radio
because the radio cared not
that we listened, but why
and to what
and this mattered

beyond the music
there was an aesthetic –
a way to listen,
an attitude for eager adolescence
identity for apt pupils
no pandering to constituents
no, just a challenge
to check this new approach
(to *sound*)
out and let that beat move us
by ourselves, together

tuning in Sunday mornings
for acoustic hangover redemption
on New Year's Eve for nostalgia
on the drive to Friday's party
to Saturday's concert
to work and the grocery store…

we'd listen and spread the word
hey did you hear that song?
yes, we did

until one day
the music
echoing the old Don McLean song
died without warning

BJ Ruddy

and a big sound machine
of disassociated charts and graphs
had control
so we turned off, tuned out
and that line was as good as any
I had to grow up
move on

Pond

Letter to My Friend's Father

To hear your daughter speak of you
you must be nothing less
than a great man

I get images of a great-grandfatherly
Walt Whitman sitting back
after a meal, always wise
the dinner table
during those fabled New England winters
must have been magic
and conversation enlightening
because it could be

I'm sure you're not perfect
I've lived at least that long
but tell me this:
I want to live up to your image for my sons
so, any bright ideas
because they're still young
and they've already seen me for a fraud
now I can't look into mirrors

I look forward to your reply

BJ Ruddy

When I Met the President

When I met the president
the night was full
with southern dinner
breaded pork chops, fried alligator,
and whiskey

Walking through Charleston
wind teased the girl's skirt
and discussions of what constitutes
"bad girl panties"
echoed through empty graveyards
of Confederate Christians
and pirates

The brown, brown, brown bar
with red glass and black leather
was midnight pond still
so we walked outside
to alive East Bay Street
and news of "Clinton's at High Cotton"

I didn't think it was worth it
but Leslie and Jean urged us to try
and once inside
drinking one fine Jack Daniel's sour
Jean pushed, adorably, through to him
and as I shook his hand
I felt OK with politics

I've got the picture
taken by his secret service guy
and that,
that was a good night

Tragedy at the Garbage Dump

The garbage dump, the busy micro metropolis in widening small town Sunday executions is common ground for classes, broken backs and books burned on tables, hurricane shelters left to air not fit to breathe, pick-up truck revivals and the minivans on the move, CB, TV, GPS, and online innovation for the eyes, imagination ostracized we'll throw it all away just don't look out at the trees – bulldozers are everywhere, dirty yellow glances behind the broken bark, breathing's what's at stake here, everyone's alive, man and son can toss the balls, their garbage pasts, these things, fifty-five degrees, it's not so bad a day to throw away the oily entourage, attendants, genius vultures, frugality on demand but not watching elections, "kill me please, my back aches, one more chair to break," standing still forever, cardboard soaking January rain, the dust of debt for mailbox paper patterned brilliant Christmas cookie state of affairs, circling cars, the garbage dump, exhaust to see, exhale, exhale, the temperature is dropping, no exit, no exit, disposal grinds it all to nothing so the heads can say it's so, this is OK, this is all good, this is something, sort of sacred, of a Sunday, soccer balls sleep flat in clean garages, look at these accomplishments, look at these achievements, treeless highway sitcoms, DVD's too big for iPod dreams, no sex in the bushes, branches breaking skin so soft for scars, the virgin in the office, doing well in a Jetta at the dump, new desk set, after Christmas sales, national anthem heartbeat, supposed to be undaunted, drinking to celebrity, pass the time but keep the place so clean (just for some him), unknown Everyman at the garbage dump – there he is, he changed his own oil too and that Civic's not that old, the boy must be his brother – a fairy tale in the making, empty out the oil, smile, car seat glances, she is not the one, but she is someone, virgin at the garbage dump, he's awake now fingers empty taking in her jeans, the rumble of a diesel and the Civic drives away, the virgin in the cooling clouds, a big wheel in the air crashes through the windshield of perception, she knows it all today – right now –

and the rest will be a letdown, lets the grease get on the steering wheel and knows what's real.

All's quiet at the garbage dump, sunset for some beers, exhaust discarded shopping trips that still show up in the mailbox, Sunday's dying there's nothing on TV she'll kill the images – where's the super-market Styrofoam? The pint of Ben & Jerry's and the wine? Where's the Civic of this heaven? Closing time, no exit, speakers hum…

Emily Dickenson's Cell Phone Rings

madness, sense, sweet divine thing
a ring-tone's whispered seduction
flowers across the airwaves
of olfactory imagination

    "what'd she want?"

nothing but, nothing but
the girl smelled like the beach
when I was seventeen

    "so what'd she want?"

I guess that's it – dial tone
no text explanation
and the hallways pass the time
in sweet motion, stairs and staring
out behind blinds

    "but what'd she want?"

it's always *always*
faraway another day
all the trips to faces talking
circles under eye lines, lazy gaze
to questions under covers
bear toes, bloodlet secrets
the history of the world

    "wait – what'd she want?"

hang-ups are inevitable
I think I have to go
to unmoved gods and frost fingers

decapitating the flowers I've imagined
while the beach walks by
out of sight

    "but…"

I can't talk right now

Cigarettes

Leaving behind cigarettes
is leaving the heart-broken lover
in the airport terminal
knowing things will never be the same
the pinch of the departure
forever to sting with wonder
about one more kiss

Or, when showing up at a friend's party
I might as well hear
"hey, where's…you know?
haven't seen her around"
true, I'll think
she's usually got a slender finger
tangled between two of mine

It will be awkward, too,
seeing the ex around town
outside of grey back doors at work
seeing her flirtatious caress
of the cheek
and strong spirit
that I'm clearly not over
being breathed in by others

True misery will be
stepping outside of a bar
to find her kissing another
drunk in the ecstasy of her breath
while I wonder
what the hell I was thinking
trying to leave all this behind
and almost reach my hand out
in "Baby, take me back" gesticulation

BJ Ruddy

But she's a bitch
too much money spent
and morning showers after late nights with her
are guilty coughs, reminders
that I have no self control

The Corner of King and Calhoun

What was it about the two kids,
college crazy, worn hoodies, jeans, flip-flops,
standing on a cool corner in low 60's February?

He was a little taller, her eyes tilted up
to look directly into his,
she, unafraid to show the fascination
his words bring.

He may have known
(may have even enjoyed it)
but he kept talking.

The opposing forces, his own mind betraying
itself in body language
as he slid his fingers up and down, up and down,
up and down the straps
of his backpack.

She was a settled dusk, low-country June,
he was the melting point of two fronts,
the hurricane's eye
might have been either of their own.

What was it about the two kids
we walked by for burritos?

So many people
out for southern Sunday slowness,
so many others,
transplants to college or Yankee refugees,
and in only a second glance
their story was clear,
the red Jeep amidst the exhaust,

BJ Ruddy

the steel, the rubber,
and there were beginnings
and endings
dependent on this moment
happening as a mixing bowl –
stick your finger in now, fine cookie dough,
and taste awareness
of the feel future nostalgia will bring
when seeing couples on corners.

She smiles but doesn't laugh,
his eyes struggle to stay on hers –
they stray to the gray ground and
he shuffles only his left foot,
fingers on the black straps,
her sweatshirt blue, his maroon.

I had an urge to take your hand and walk
like couples are supposed to,
pretty on the outside,
so Hallmark would be jealous and
The Saturday Evening Post would exhume
Norman Rockwell (a comeback
no aging rockers could touch)
for us and our hands and our eyes.

On the corner, their breath is tangible,
humid August born into revealing February;
words, even to them, are completely insignificant,
as they'll only know the corner
and their eyes –
they may even forget the sweatshirts
but born was a feeling
Wordsworth would admire,
as whatever moved forward,
would do so from *this* spot,
the points two roads diverged

Pond

(converged, emerged) from.

They'll have this, even if they lose each other…

Even if I did take your hand,
it would only be pretense;
our thing is not something displayed
and what it is poems only insult;
ours is not the flippant hand-hold,
however nice, because
distance equals a cool closeness,
and present tense nostalgia
is never physical, not us…

She reached up and took his hands,
she, almost – her only indecisive second –
reached her lips to kiss…

They moved from the corner,
towards Marion Square, hand in hand…

What was it about the two kids
and their moment?

I did not take your hand
but I looked at your left,
the fingers I've always been so transfixed by,
the thin electric length,
and there I was able to go back
to our corner,
that dim-lit Jersey bar
with indie-rock and smoke,
and that coffee house, outside,
with red candles and cheap plastic table cloths,
flimsy white chairs and your smile
rapidly expounding self-descriptions
as I inhaled you in August Atlantic humidity.

BJ Ruddy

The two kids (college crazy) knew,
didn't know, unlearned, absorbed,
like the imprinting of history,
documentation on the mind,
so that someday, somewhere,
this might make its meaning
warm…

Construction Site

Rain
clay, concrete
two men duck for a smoke
"That's to be the front door"
I think, driving past

BJ Ruddy

The Old Mercedes

The old diesel Mercedes has worn tires
so in rain they worry about the child
still in his car seat, watching the movie screen window
while discussions of money haunt the music
that would otherwise be the gentle background voices
supposed to be soothing to a daydreaming mind

To get cyclical conversation off of his mind
he attempts to reach across a hand, but tires
as if other cars on this highway were warning voices
and any movement of his could disrupt the child
not in the car seat, but the one hearing the music
while she stared in escape at the movie screen window

There is a top to bottom crack in her window
and she whispers absent dreams that come to mind
because she has learned to hate this song, his music
wearing on her like his worn sweaters, like the car's tires
but things, as they say, are complicated – the child
knows the meaning of words is nothing to the sound of voices

He knows his tone and she is silenced in voices
that only remind her that there's no exit in this window
and what could be worse for him, for the child
could she really ever get either off of her mind
like when he plays the Allmans, she pictures the tires
spin-cycle overdue bills as if soap was in music

He knows they've stopped talking and that she hates the music
but is it worse than the heat of claustrophobic voices
that can never get back the miles that've worn these old tires
that can never refresh the view from this pollen stained window
that have lost the meaning of words in projections of mind
all in the so called protection of that car seat's child

Pond

And how in the world was it that she bore him this child
not so long ago when waves washed the only music
and a few lonely sea gulls' songs of love filled her mind
flying low in their freedom the gods in their voices
they were outside in the night, a beach without this window
that she's drawn back to again with the hum of the tires

He knows that she knows her mind will always be in this child
and that someday these tires will fade away with this music
but for now they've their voices and the view from this window

C.

He is not so much boy
anymore
but he is the boy
who is savior
and reason

Because now in sheets
under tan walls
with bureaus and
a ceiling fan I installed
identity is
the next letter,
C

In spring pools
winter thin turns
to summer muscle
and I see him later
leaving me to
return to autumn dust

Without responsibility
there are two males
who exist with
the same last name
but the audacity
to use cutting tones
is the thing
that makes that true

A child that knows who I am
is a better man than I

Pond

www.ingramcontent.com/pod-product-compliance
Lightning Source LLC
Chambersburg PA
CBHW032042040426
42449CB00007B/982